D1608371

WARBIRDS ILLUSTRATED NO. 26

Air War over Vietnam

Volume IV   DANA BELL

ARMS AND ARMOUR PRESS
London—Melbourne—Harrisburg, Pa.—Cape Town

Introduction

Warbirds Illustrated 26: Air War over Vietnam Volume IV
Published in 1984 by Arms and Armour Press,
Lionel Leventhal Limited, 2–6 Hampstead High
Street, London NW3 1QQ; 4–12 Tattersalls Lane,
Melbourne, Victoria 3000, Australia; Sanso Centre,
8 Adderley Street, P.O. Box 94, Cape Town 8000;
Cameron and Kelker Streets, P.O. Box 1831,
Harrisburg, Pennsylvania 17105, USA

British Library Cataloguing in Publication Data:
Bell, Dana
Air War over Vietnam.—(Warbirds illustrated; 26)
1. Vietnamese Conflict, 1961–1975—Aerial
operations, American—Pictorial works
I. Title   II. Series
959.704′348   DS558.8
ISBN 0–85368–635–1

Edited by Michael Boxall.
Layout by Roger Chesneau.
Printed and bound in Great Britain by William
Clowes Limited, Beccles and London.

For this full-colour pictorial survey of US air
involvement in the Vietnam War, I have chosen
photographs which I hope will convey to the
reader the special atmosphere of that difficult
combat environment, as well as provide him with a
general overview of the major aircraft types used
there.

The photographs for this volume have come
primarily from official sources, especially the
public affairs office of the US Air Force to whom
I extend my thanks.

Dana Bell, Virginia, 1984

◀3
Cover illustration: A Phantom (foreground) and
two Thunderchiefs queue up for refuelling from a
KC-135 (USAF)
1. (Half-title page) With fire suppression bottle
suspended at the ready, an HH-43B patrols near Da
Nang Air Base in November 1966. (USAF)
2. (Title spread) A VF-96 F-4B Phantom firing
underwing rockets at a Viet Cong stronghold in
April 1965. (USN)
3. The setting sun is reflected off rice paddies on the
Ca Mau peninsula as a USAF A-1E returns from a
strike. (USAF)

▲4
4. Visiting C-119s line the ramp at Bangkok, Thailand, during Operation 'Firm Link', February 1956. Thai, Philippine, and US services mounted a show of force which failed to impress Communist leaders in Cambodia, Laos, or Vietnam. (USAF)

▼5

5. F-84Gs of the 49th Fighter-Bomber Wing are made ready for a mission during 'Firm Link'. (USAF)
6. A Thai security policeman guards an F-100D of the 35th TFS during 'Airlink', a 1957 exercise in Bangkok. (USAF)

7. Thai workers unload supplies from a C-130A at Bangkok during the Laos crisis of 1959. Red tail and wing markings were worn by US transports when flying over arctic, desert, or jungle regions. (USAF)
8. New Zealand was also interested in keeping South-East Asia peaceful. Airmen of 41 Squadron stand by for inspection with one of their Bristol Freighters during a display in Thailand, June 1962. (USAF)
9. Ten years later, a camouflaged RNZAF Bristol delivers military cargo to South Vietnam. (Via Mesko)

▼7

8▲ 9▼

▲10 ▼11

10. A Royal Australian Air Force Sabre is refuelled as the ground crew and pilot prepare for joint exercises. (USAF)
11. The first 'Ranch Hand' defoliation aircraft arrived in South Vietnam in January 1962. US Defense Department planners, after conferring with President Kennedy, decided that no attempt would be made to disguise the purpose of the aircraft. (USAF)
12. Initial 'Ranch Hand' missions were designed to remove the ground cover used by the Viet Cong and North Vietnamese when ambushing South Vietnamese road and rail transport. Here a C-123 sprays defoliant beside a Vietnamese highway. (USAF)
13. Martin B-57Bs of the 3rd Bomb Wing line a South Vietnamese Air Base in 1965. Red noses, tail letters, and fuselage stripes identified the 13th Tactical Bomb Squadron, while yellow marked the 8th TBS. (USAF)

▲14

▲15 ▼16

14. As the air war escalated, Tactical Air Command units were transferred from the US to Pacific Air Forces (PACAF) control. This B-66 at Tan Son Nhut, Saigon in 1965 still carries its TAC shield and lightning bolt on the tail. (USAF)

15. A C-118A prepares to transfer casualties from Tan Son Nhut during heavy rains in 1965. (USAF)

16. The camouflage of this RF-101C was the result of a series of experiments conducted on US-based tactical aircraft in 1963 and 1964. By 1965, the Voodoo had also seen many internal modifications to improve photographic capability and combat survivability. (USAF)

17. Two more Tan Son Nhut RF-101Cs display both the standardized TAC camouflage (with small national insignia) and the earlier experimental camouflage, with its oversized US star. (USAF)

18. Napalm canisters beneath the wings of USAF A-1Es during operations in 1964. (USAF)

19. 'Linda', a C-123 from a US Pacific Air Forces (PACAF) troop carrier unit, in 1964. (USAF)

17▲

18▲ 19▼

▲20

20. Unbuttoned for maintenance, a Vertol CH-21 stands in the sun at Tan Son Nhut in 1964. The aircraft was probably assigned to the 145th Aviation Battalion, which had assumed control of several light helicopter companies during the previous year. The three-toned camouflage is similar to a scheme adopted by the USAF. (USAF)

21. A 1st Air Commando Squadron A-1E prepares for takeoff from Pleiku Air Base in the Vietnamese Central Highlands near Cambodia in 1966. The original Navy light gull grey and white colours are obvious, but the original tail markings have been replaced by USAF-style codes. (USAF)

22. An assortment of camouflaged and aluminium finish 4th TFW F-105Ds on the flight line at Takhli AB, Thailand in December 1965. (USAF)

21▲

22▼

▲23 ▼24

25 ▲

26 ▲

23. South Vietnamese A-1Hs in dark brown and green camouflage in 1965. The only national insignia is a small Vietnamese flag on the rudders. (USAF)
24. A 750lb bomb is delivered to an F-100D of the 308th TFS early in 1966. (USAF)

25. South Vietnamese paratroopers tumble from a C-123 during a training exercise in April 1966. (USAF)
26. A Douglas EF-10B of VMCJ-1 landing after a mission to record North Vietnamese radio communications. (USAF)

28 ◄

29 ▲

27. (Previous spread) A long exposure captures the motion of maintenance vehicles along the F-100 revetments of the 481st TFS at Tan Son Nhut, July 1968. (USAF)
28. F-4Bs of Marine Fighter-Attack Squadrons 323 and 115 refuelling at the Da Nang hardstand in January 1966. (USAF)
29. Two stars on the door mark this C-47B as the personal aircraft of General Vin Loch, commander of the Vietnamese II Corps. The photograph was taken at the general's headquarters at Pleiku Air Base in 1966. (USAF)
30. T-6 trainers of the Royal Thai Air Force sit on the hardstand at Korat, 1967. (USAF)

30 ▼

▲31 ▼32

33▲

31. A 429th TFS F-100D *en route* to a Vietnamese target in December 1965. Note the mission symbols on the nose of the aircraft. (USAF)

32. Royal Thai F-86Ls fly formation with a USAF TF-102A during a joint training mission over Thailand in 1966. (USAF)

33. Two 509th Fighter Interceptor Squadron F-102As patrol the skies of South Vietnam in November 1967. (USAF)

34. A black-bellied 8th TFW F-4D has its weapons armed at the 'last chance' checkpoint prior to a September 1972 mission. Alongside is a Royal Thai Air Force T-28. (USAF)

34▼

▲35

35. Its wing set at a high angle of attack, a US Marine Corps F-8E takes off from Da Nang. All-weather Fighter Squadron 235, April 1966. (USAF)

36. Ordnance crews remove 20mm ammunition from the wings of a Navy A-1H after a wheels-up landing at Da Nang in December 1965. (USAF)

37. With external fuel tanks and an ALQ-99 electronic counter-measures pod beneath its wings, a Marine EA-6A prepares for take-off at Da Nang in June 1970. The eagle and lightning bolt insignia belongs to the 1st Composite Reconnaissance Squadron (VMCJ-1). (USAF)

38. Revetted at Da Nang in late 1966, these F-4Cs show their hastily applied camouflage. The original white bellies with large insignia have not been repainted in light grey, and chipped upper-surface paint shows the original light gull grey. (USAF)

39. An airman of the 355th TFW retouches the paint on one of his unit's Republic F-105Ds at Takhli AB, Thailand, 1966. (USAF)

▼36

37 ▲

38 ▲   39 ▼

▲40 ▼41

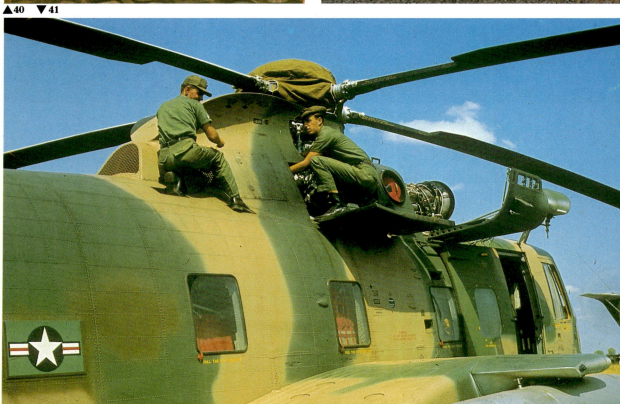

40. A member of the 56th Combat Support Group sprays paint on an HH-3E of Detachment 1, 40th Aerospace Rescue & Recovery Squadron (ARRS) at Nakhon Phanom AB (known as 'NKP' or 'Naked Fanny' by US crews), Thailand, February 1969. (USAF)
41. Men of the 30th ARRS work on the jet engine and transmission of an HH-3C Jolly Green Giant, Udorn AB, Thailand, 1966. (USAF)

42. A Sikorsky HH-3E from Detachment 1, 40th ARRS, stands on the flightline at Nakhon Phanom AB, Thailand in early 1969. The symbols indicating successful missions are stencilled on the fuselage behind the pilot's seat. (USAF)
43. Seen from the open cargo ramp of an HC-130, an HH-53C takes on fuel. Note the pintle-mounted mini-gun in the 'Dutch door' behind the helicopter's pilot. (USAF)

43 ▼

 44

44. A camouflaged A-1E sweeps over the Vietnamese jungle during a rescue mission. By 1967, Skyraiders claimed the highest overall loss rate of any aircraft in the theatre – as high as 6.2 per thousand sorties over North Vietnam. (USAF)

45. HC-130s served for command, control, and communications (C^3 or 'Cee-cubed') during rescue missions, with some models providing air-to-air refuelling for HH-3s and HH-53s. HC-130Ps, as seen here, were converted from HC-130Hs and retained the earlier aircraft's Fulton aerial recovery equipment on the nose. The Fulton equipment was never successfully used in South-East Asia. (USAF)

46. Camouflaged to effect, an HC-130P refuels an HH-53C over the Vietnamese countryside. Note the mismatched engine nacelles. (USAF)

47. Only a few USAF HU-16 Albatrosses received this dark blue/white camouflage scheme. Note the wide overspray between the colours. Da Nang, April 1966. (USAF)

▼45

▲48 ▼49

48. Gloss black O-2As, which flew night air-control missions along the Ho Chi Minh Trail, wait on the Nakhon Phanom ramp, 1970. (USAF)

49. The sinister-looking canisters being fitted to the racks of this A-1E carry Spikebuoy sensors to be dropped and planted along the Ho Chi Minh Trail. As part of Project 'Igloo White', the Spikebuoys automatically radioed signals triggered by the vibrations of passing traffic. Nakhon Phanom AB, Thailand, June 1968. (USAF)

50. Flames at the Ubon runway mark the site of the first AC-130A combat loss. Hit by 37mm ground fire over Laos, the gunship returned home with one man dead; a second crewman was killed in the crash, 24 May 1969. (USAF)

50 ▼

▲51 ▼52

51. An overhauled T56-A turboprop is mounted on an AC-130A of the 16th SOS at Ubon AB, Thailand. The unmatched cowling panels are unlikely to be repainted before operations resume. (USAF)

52. An AC-130A's turboprop engine is removed at a Ubon revetment, June 1969. (USAF)

53. Pave Aegis was the ultimate weapons modification to the AC-130E Spectre gunship – the aftmost 40mm gun was replaced by an Army 105mm howitzer! The throw weight of each round went from 0.6lb to 5.6lb, greatly increasing the chance of destroying a given target while keeping the gunship at a high, safer altitude. (USAF)

54. In position aboard the gunship, final adjustments are made to the howitzer. Flare launchers can be seen in the right foreground. (USAF)

55. An airborne battlefield command and control centre (ABCCC) is inserted into the cargo area of a C-130 at Udorn in late 1971. The pod can be switched to another C-130 during normal aircraft maintenance periods. (USAF)

53 ▲

54 ▲ 55 ▼

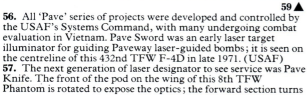

59 ▲

60 ▲

56. All 'Pave' series of projects were developed and controlled by the USAF's Systems Command, with many undergoing combat evaluation in Vietnam. Pave Sword was an early laser target illuminator for guiding Paveway laser-guided bombs; it is seen on the centreline of this 432nd TFW F-4D in late 1971. (USAF)
57. The next generation of laser designator to see service was Pave Knife. The front of the pod on the wing of this 8th TFW Phantom is rotated to expose the optics; the forward section turns upward to protect the lens from dust or gravel. Ubon AB, 1973. (USAF)
58. The smaller, lighter Pave Spike pod could be mounted in a forward Sparrow bay of a Phantom. Pave Spike has remained in service into the 1980s. (USAF)
59. Exposed optics for Pave Spike. 1973. (USAF)
60. Close-up of the Paveway sight mounted in the rear cockpit of an F-4. (USAF)

▲ 61

61. A US Navy UH-1E lands beside an Army UH-1B on USS *Harnett County* (LST-821) between combat operations in the Mekong Delta. Co Chien River, October 1967. (USN)

62. 1st Air Cavalry troopers arrive by C-130A at Bu Dup Special Forces Camp, during the Cambodian Offensive, May 1970. (USAF)

63. Following a saturation bombing by B-52s in 1966, US Army troopers begin a search and destroy mission as their UH-1D prepares to leave. (USAF)

▲ 64

▲ 65   ▼ 66

64. A Vietnamese Air Force A-1E flies over a 'hootch line' and fortified hamlet in 1964. The US Navy serial number remains on the tail, though the aircraft is painted in an overall grey scheme used by the USAF. (USAF)

65. Maintenance on a turboprop engine of an OV-10 Forward Air Control (FAC) aircraft, Da Nang, September 1970. (USAF)

66. Carrying four marker rockets, a Vietnamese O-1 FAC flies to its patrol area. (USAF)

67. Safety-pins are removed from the bombs and rockets on a pair of VNAF A-37s, Da Nang, September 1970. (USAF)

68. High above South Vietnam, a Canberra of 2 Squadron, RAAF, heads for a strike in March 1970. The Australian unit was based at Phan Rang AB, South Vietnam. (USAF)

69. A handsomely marked A-37 rests in its Vietnamese revetment, September 1969. (USAF)

67▲

68▲ 69▼

▲70 ▼71

70. A foam-covered F-4C is raised at Bien Hoa in February 1966. Note how the underwing fuel tanks, which protected the lower fuselage and wings, have ruptured and punctured the outboard wing flaps. (USAF)
71. Loaded with napalm canisters, a VNAF A-1H tucks its landing gear away and leaves Da Nang, October 1966. (USAF)

72. A number of Phantoms had light grey painted over tan areas of their camouflage. Though this 16th TRS RF-4C was photographed at Tan Son Nhut in late 1967, other examples were seen in Germany and the USA. (USAF)
73. An Air Force cameraman adjusts his G-suit before boarding a 388th TFW Phantom at Korat AB, June 1970. (USAF)

72 ▲

73 ▼

▲ 74

74. Behind a forward catapult aboard USS *America*, an E-2A airborne warning and control aircraft is prepared for its next mission. Across the flight deck, an armed A-6 also awaits orders. September 1970. (USAF)

75. An F-4J of Fighter Squadron 31 returns to USS *Saratoga* following an August 1972 MiG CAP (combat air patrol). (USAF)

76. Armourers load Pave Pat, a sinister-looking fuel-air explosive, onto the wing rack of a 1st SOS A-1E, September 1968. (USAF)

75 ▶

▲77

▲78

77. 750lb bombs are attached to the MER (Multiple Ejector Rack) of a 428th TFS F-111A before one of the first 'Combat Lancer' missions in March 1968. (USAF)

78. Prior to 'Combat Lancer' (the first deployment of F-111As to South-East Asia) red, white, and blue stripes are painted on the nose of the Detachment Commander's aircraft. 428th TFS, March 1968. (USAF)

79. F-111As returned to combat in September 1972, but encountered a number of critical parts shortages and maintenance problems; seven of fifty-two aircraft were lost. Nevertheless, the 429th TFS (shown) and the 430th TFS flew more than 3,000 missions prior to the signing of the Paris Peace Accords in 1973. (USAF)

80. An F-111A of the 430th TFS out of Takhli, photographed during the unit's last combat mission on 15 August 1973. (USAF)

81. A USAF sergeant checks the 20mm Vulcan gun of a Thailand-based F-105D. A red star stencilled below the cockpit credits the aircraft with one North Vietnamese MiG destroyed. (USAF)
82. An A-1H of Attack Squadron 115 returns to USS *Kitty Hawk* after a strike against the Viet Cong in 1966. (USAF)
83. An A-1E tests the BAK-12 arresting gear at Nakhon Phanom, Thailand in October 1970. Note the black-bellied H-3 and C-123 in the background. (USAF)
84. When the Air National Guard's 188th TFS was activated and ordered to South Vietnam, it came under control of the 31st TFW. One of the squadron's F-100Cs banks over Tuy Hoa before landing. (USAF)
85. High over South Vietnam, an F-100D of the 306th TFS carries two 500lb high drag bombs (outboard racks), two fuel tanks (centre racks), and a pair of napalm bombs (inboard racks). (USAF)

81 ▶

82 ▶

83 ▲

84 ▲   85 ▼

▲86 ▼87

86. Maintenance crews install a J-71 engine on an EB-66 of the 41st Tactical Electronic Warfare Squadron (TEWS) at Takhli, Thailand, September 1969. (USAF)

87. A 42nd TEWS (attached to the 355th TFW) EB-66 approaches a KC-135 for refuelling, March 1970. (USAF)

88. A Strategic Air Command KC-135 climbs out of U-Tapao AB, Thailand, on an aerial refuelling mission, 1970. (USAF)

89. UH-1Ps were flown by the USAF on psychological warfare missions and air base defence activities. 1967. (USAF)

90. MiG combat air patrol. A formation of 33rd TFW F-4Es and 432nd TRW F-4Ds patrol for enemy jets. Missiles, guns, and ECM pods for air-to-air combat can be seen in this 1972 photograph. (USAF)

88 ▲

89 ▲   90 ▼

91. Hercules transports provided much of Australia's heavy airlift support. (Via Mesko)

92. An SH-3 hovers over the fantail of the US destroyer *Benner* off the coast of Vietnam. (USAF)

93. Although the overall engine grey scheme was a standard for Navy SH-3s, most of the Sea Kings carried high-visibility markings and insignia. The story behind this duller scheme is unknown. (USAF)

91►

▼92

▲ 94

▲ 95 ▼ 96

94. An F-4J of Marine Fighter-Attack Squadron 542 taxis out of Da Nang, May 1966. (USAF)
95. The Republic of Korea sent troops to Vietnam, but left the air war to the USAF and VNAF. Although this red and white Cessna Skymaster was used in support of the Koreans, it is not certain in what role. (Via Mesko)

96. Following a December 1968 mission over South Vietnam, two 557th TFS F-4Cs return to Cam Ranh Bay AB. (USAF)
97. A Grumman S-2C target tug aircraft stands at the catapult prior to launch from USS *Bennington*. (USAF)
98. An RC-135D, used to collect electronic Intelligence data, approaches a KC-135 for refuelling, January 1967. (USAF)

99. UH-1Bs of the 101st Airborne Division are offloaded from a Military Airlift Command C-133 at Tan Son Nhut Air Base. Elements of the 'Screamin' Eagles' had previously fought in Vietnam, but in late 1967 the entire division arrived during operation 'Eagle Thrust'. (USAF)

100. The long shadows of a late December afternoon wash this Lockheed C-130A near Cam Ranh Bay in 1966. (USAF)

101. A Huey of the US Army's 1st Aviation Brigade lifts off from Tan Son Nhut Air Base in May 1970. The 1st, one of the largest commands in South Vietnam, had been headquartered at Tan Son Nhut before moving to Long Binh in December 1967. (USAF)

102. An Air Force sergeant – wearing 'uniform of the day' for Thailand – paints the canopy rail of a 307th TFS Phantom in the squadron colour. Air and ground crew names would be stencilled on the left and right sides respectively. Udorn AB, October 1972. (USAF)

101 ▲ 102 ▼

103. With its US Army markings overpainted, this patchwork C-7A and its US Air Force crew prepare to leave Phu Cat in June 1967. (USAF)

104. The Strategic Air Command's 99th Aerial Refueling Squadron took their 'Ramrod' callsign seriously – it could be found painted on the forward fuselage of most of the unit's KC-135s. (USAF)

105. Troops search for survivors at the crash site of a UH-1D near the Cambodian border in December 1968. (USAF)

106. Pilot and Weapons Systems Operator of a 58th TFS F-4E deplane at Udorn AB, Thailand in late 1972. Spreader bars allow each bomb rack to carry two Sidewinders in addition to the normal three-bomb load. (USAF)

▲103 ▼104

▼105   106▶

▲107

▲108 ▼109

107. 20mm Vulcan gun pods move to Vietnam with the 49th TFW in May 1972 as part of the US response to the North Vietnamese spring offensive. (USAF)

108. Members of the 49th TFW prepare their F-4Ds for deployment to South-East Asia in May 1972. (USAF)

109. Refuelling high over Thailand, an A-7D of the 354th TFW engages the boom of a KC-135 tanker. Coloured segments of the boom help the boom operator (known as the 'boomer' or 'gas-passer') to gauge the distance between the two aircraft. (USAF)

110. Engine start at dusk for an A-26K at Nakhon Phanom. The bottom of the aircraft, as well as its load of napalm bombs, has been painted black for night operations. (USAF)

111. Bombs are loaded aboard a B-52D at U-Tapao AB, Thailand, in September 1972. (USAF)

112. (Overleaf)A-7Ds of the 354th TFW disappear against the camouflaged hardstand at Korat AB, Thailand, October 1972. (USAF)

▲113

▲114

113. An F-4E of the 421st TFS prepares for its final bombing mission of the Vietnam War, 15 August 1973. (USAF)

114. A sharkmouthed 388th TFW F-105 is prepared for the trip home as the wing redeploys from Thailand to the USA in August 1973. (USAF)

115. Credited with three MiG kills as an F-105F, this aircraft was modified to an F-105G for 'Wild Weasel' anti-SAM missions with

the 561st TFS. Photographed at Korat AB, Thailand before returning to the USA in August 1973, the same aircraft is now part of the US Air Force Museum collection at Wright-Patterson AFB, Ohio. (USAF)

116. An A-26K of the 609th Special Operations Squadron sweeps over flooded plains near Nakhon Phanom AB, Thailand July 1969. (USAF)

▲117

▲118

▲119 ▼120

117. The President of the Philippines arrives at Clark Air Base in his Fokker F-27 to greet repatriated US POWs. The Americans were interviewed and given medical examinations at the US base in the Philippines prior to being shipped home. (USAF)

118. 'Enhance Plus' was an accelerated re-supply effort to help South Vietnamese forces fill the vacuum left by the withdrawing Americans. A VNAF C-123K taxis past C-130As at Tan Son Nhut following a hasty transfer. November 1972. (USAF)

119. Additional reconnaissance was provided by AQM-34 drones, which were launched and controlled by DC-130 Hercules aircraft. Udorn, 8 April 1975. (USAF)

120. April 1975 was the last month of two separate Vietnams. As the final North Vietnamese campaign began, this U-2R reconnaissance plane was photographed at U-Tapao AB, Thailand. The yellow stand in the foreground gives access to the cockpit while providing shade from the sun. (USAF)